By W. Scott

OWL'S NEST
PUBLISHERS

OWL'S NEST
PUBLISHERS

Est. 2021
Owl's Nest Publishers
P. O. Box 63
Cross Plains, WI 53528
owlsnestpublishers.com

Cover Design & Images: Ash Schlax
Section Images: Ash Schlax
Title Font(s): Ash Schlax / Black Mango Thin
Text Font: Times New Roman

ISBN: 978-1-957362-07-6 (paperback)

Muses from the Moon / by W. Scott
muses from the moon is a collection of poetry, split into four sections, that
detail the trials of struggling faith.

Printed in the United States of America

Books by W. Scott

Bottled Messages:
  Post-Its and Parchment
  Notecards and Scrolls
  Postcards and Bristol

for those tired, withering and brave souls

that keep searching for the light.

prologue

once, someone told me that the moon cannot
shine on its own.

and it got me thinking about how in our relationship
with Christ, we cannot shine—we are unable to do anything
without Him.

many decades ago, scholars of the world believed that our planet
was the center of the universe.

how wrong was that theory!

it wasn't until years later
scientists confirmed that the earth
actually orbits around the sun.

and like us, in our relationship with Jesus,
He is our center.

muses from the moon
is a collection of struggling faith,
a holding on in the dark,
well, not truly dark because,
like the moon
needing the glow of the sun,
and like humanity,
formed in the image of our Father,
being made new into the image of our Savior,
and the very essence of us being in constant need
of His light,

His light, His light, His light,
is always available to us

if we would just keep
looking.

new moon

ghost town

around the edges everything is
hazy.

the language of butterfly fingers.
the heavy as it tightrope walks
around your throat.
the need to make the poem work,
to fit the hem just right.

but doesn't.

when everything unravels, it is
molasses slow.

listen closely to how the moon dips
and becomes eggshells.
how you wrap your hand around a
familiar waist but it no
longer takes root.

the way your own mouth becomes a
ghost town.

and Lord, will it always feel like
this?

will it always feel as if
something is ending?

depression and antidepressants

if you are reading this, know that there isn't
anything whole.

not the onset of the day
as it quietly tiptoes. not joy glistening between
a passing strangers teeth. not even the heat
in a loved one's hand.

and the only conclusion is this —

i must have forgotten myself somewhere
(again).

i am quiet,
but you see,

there is a trail of blood.

are we or are we not

what a cruel fate it is.

to be given hands to chase the light.
but never being able to catch it.

are we or are we not meant
to crave possibilities?

or will it always start out ugly?
will it be salt in the wounds?

can the door that is constantly slamming
be a mistake?

i write in mostly question marks.
and open-ended phrases.

and i fill every corner of the house
with them.

still, no one thinks to question
the silence.

or to understand.

worst kind of strange

it isn't enough. it is the worst
kind of strange.

this heart is burdensome in
nature.

a car crash. falling art.
a cruel kind of fate.

i cannot remember the last time i
had come up for air.

because more often than not,
i spend the nights with fingers
curled. and lips that trip over
every vowel and prayer.

the explanation:
i am trying to come to terms
with this.

that even in this rich stark
quiet,

love is still being poured out
like a seattle rain.

9

(this is the human in us)

except that the moon is coming
undone.

(and it is for a good reason).

we dare not to avert our eyes.

(this is the human in us).

every breath flutters.
every breath pirouettes.
unsteadily. becomes the tipping point.

and this is the best-kept secret:

we let the poems grow jagged.
we've decided to let them sharpen
our teeth.

chuckle at all of the metaphors,
those that cause us the most
discomfort.

like, how anxiety grows into
tide pools that spill into
something bigger,

which is to simply say
that we've grown used to all
of the agony.

every. brutal. fist.

reach

what does anyone know,
really, of a heart

that is partially slumbering?

of the moments
you choose to reach,

and dig the weeds out of
the concrete?

waterlogged

each of my prayers have become waterlogged.

they are splintering and wet
empty land.

once, i opened my jaw,
but my mouth cracked and stood
still.

(does this mean anything? are the words
too far gone?)

i breathe but i am unsure of the source.

shipwreck

we sit on a ledge in our own
thoughts / contemplate the expanse /

the sinking / the stretch
for miles and miles /

and the stillness / this unruly air /

it is a shipwreck /

and we are the ship / meaning
the precipice is inviting /

meaning there are heels
moving / meaning *i* am moving /

wait, no, no, i am not sure /

yes, yes / i am moving /

there is heat now / and before
the jump /

i breathe /

and it is slow / like moonrise /
like smoke and the last bit of honey /

here is the fall /

and i am not frightened /

blade

in the dark, i've held my own hand.
and have only ever known it as a blade.

when i say this

but
i had already been
open-mouthed.

i had already been
standing here,

hands folded
and screaming.

tucked away my little heart
underneath floorboards.

let the grief
have its way
and hollow me out.

know that when i say this,
there isn't always going to be
poetry here.

a midnight walk up west fourth street

admittedly, the night is a wolf.
all stretched claws and prowling.

i know that i should be
afraid. every vein within me should
be a tidal wave of fear.

but isn't.

these days, i leave a voicemail,
but it is more smoke,

more spilled blood
than comfort.

more of me trying to write to you
with my left hand
instead of my right.

do you understand?

i walk the streets at night.
the pavement is wet
but the rain no longer makes music.

which is to say that
when i tell you that my heart
is caged and the night is a padlock,
be truthful with me
and tell me,

is there anything left
to be desired?

war

and then i think that maybe there are wars
that we are just not meant to
overcome.

if i am honest (and that is what i'm
trying to be) maybe i just don't
care if i am alright. maybe feeling

like shattered glass
in the kitchen sink
is home.

i don't care to be something sticky
sweet. no one ever counted or bottled
my tears to understand. and they never
warmed a home.

so if i am honest, maybe i will
choose not to finish these three
books. maybe i will let the poems
become ash on my fingertips. maybe i
do not believe that i will make it past
winter.

not sure

the lyrics are heavy. like early
morning manhattan smog.

which means the metaphors are a
paperweight.

which means the paperweight sits
on my chest.

which means evening has arrived and
i'm drowning.

no one knows that i've spent the
day like expensive glassware
sitting on the edge of an end
table.

this is that black-cold side of
the moon that nobody sees.

maybe you've heard of it from a
distance.

the beat. beat. beating.

a pulse.

once, someone told me that it was
because i am still alive.

but inwardly,
i am just not sure.

i know love

what would you say
if i asked you for
permission to be open?

to share my grief
at the dinner table?

would the conversation
only be swollen
tender-thick quiet?

say that i noticed your angry
chest. your tight lips.

and all i see is the weapon.

you, eyes closed, listen to
the sound of skin peeling
off of the back of my palm.

you say love is messy.
you say it dips and swings.

i say i've known love.
some of the greatest love.

and it has only ever
spit me back out onto the pavement.

at five

if you were to go back
a few years, a five-year-old
little boy stands unsure
and tight-fisted on the
grassy plains of
liberty state park.

he clutches his blue and yellow
charlie brown kite,
a most prized possession.

at five, he feels the winds
echo angrily. they whip
and turn and whisper.
the little boy knows
that the winds are pushed by force.
he knows that the breeze is hungry.

standing next to him is the man
he once knew as his father,
his strong tower, his mighty
protection.

on his kite,
the little boy's grip never slips.
he loved his kite. but when he saw
his stepfather give the nod of
approval, when he felt the wind
push and howl from the east,
he knew that it was time.

the boy and his
stepfather turned their gaze
towards the heavens.

slowly, he uncurled his tiny
fingers from around the

bunched-up tether.

and immediately, the kite took flight.
immediately, the little boy felt
the wind's growling hunger and he
wanted to scream for his father's
help.

Those few moments felt like
an eternity,
wading alone amongst the windswept
plains, his stepfather's guidance

absent.

the five-year-old boy struggled alone,
fighting the groaning gale that
wanted his beloved kite.

but he would not let the heavens have it.
he would not.
he could not.

the boy looked up at the changing, dejected
expanse and prayed to the only God he knew
that the coming tempest would have mercy;

his small delicate, fingers drenched
in anxious sweat, the charlie brown
kite inching further and further away
with each passing second.

grey clouds moved in
and the little boy wondered out loud,

what if...what if God doesn't like my kite
so close to him, what if he shoots it down?

his stepfather, taken aback for a moment,

could only stand behind his boy
as grey clouds rushed in further.

he watched his son struggle, letting
his question twirl and melt within the
recesses of his own thoughts.

softly, the stepfather gripped the
little boy's tiny fingers, wrapping his own
around the kite's string.

the stepfather answered,

God would never do that.

and even though the little boy heard his father's
answer, an acknowledgment that was supposed to be
a well of comfort, a place of a soft landing,
he also heard his trepidation.

the little boy looked up to the heavens
once more, watched as his kite
whipped and twirled haphazardly against
the winds, said a small and what he believed
to be an insignificant prayer

yet words that meant the most to him
in that hour,

trying to hold on to and digest his
father's words of faith,

he let go of the kite's tail entirely
and watched his treasures float away.

not knowing

my wrists are,
if not more,
an unsteady thing.

when i stretch myself
thin in the quiet,

when my feet run
of their own volition,

and yet, i still look
for you in the shadows.

wonder if there is
still more time.

and
my lord,
this humanness.

(and its way of not knowing
how to cling to the good things.)

so i beat my chest
instead.

wait for you like
the next breath.

a heartbeat.

your love is something
that i could never truly
understand.

flatline

there isn't an answer here.
when the end arrives,
it is monday.

right here,
the current is flatline.
and the world?
they see the door slam.
they hear the locks click.

today, we are accustomed
to angry tongues.
we've come to know the bottom
only as desire.

but when every wound grows,
when they stretch from one end
to the next, and no one thinks
about questioning the silence,

how do we dare to still call it love?

conversations with the therapist

i say there are stories. and then
there are stories.

i say, there, i see a glimmer of the moon. but fear
still holds me. i say that i've seen the worst of it.

lived it. became it.

but how do you see yourself, asks the therapist.

i begin. i begin again.

but don't.

my wrists sit quietly in my lap.

but i begin. in my thoughts mostly.
how do i see myself?

it isn't written letter. or a good laugh
at my own expense.

not a pick of the lock (because there isn't any key).

it isn't morning song.
or something stolen.

not bruises from holding onto the railing (because i don't
always reach for it).

it isn't plucked
ripe berries from the vine.

or decades of familiar skin.
or only being indoor storm.
or crack of lightning.

or breathing and breathing and breathing...

how do you see yourself?

i begin. and i begin again.
i say, *nothing*.

phases

the language of who i am
has always been tentative.

i am a different kind of tongue.
radio static. the snap of a tree limb
that nobody hears. roots
untwining.

didn't you hear that in the distance?
i didn't think so.

maybe like light,
i will fade with the wind.

wane with every season.

purple hyacinth

did you know that i've tried

to crack open the sky for five
long years now?

i even ripped up every purple
hyacinth from the garden.

the ones that i planted with tears.

when i said, *here.*
these are for you.

but it's like you heard my voice. but would not
open the clouds.

do you understand now?

everything is too hot.
everything is too cold.
everything is too heavy.
everything is.

i am trying. i am so, so trying.

any other way

this is the song
from the belly
of a storm that
continues to
tear and
split.

sharp notes scattered.
a gift of pressed edges.

because i want to know
if you truly understand.

this is purposeful, tangible pain.
and it's not that i want you to suffer
with me.

it's just that i have no idea
how to cry for help
any other way.

what we need

most of the time, we sweep through
like an unfinished story.

we grow attached to all of
the hard that lives on the edge
of fingertips.

and we believe that it is for
good reason.

after all, we've dug and planted
but nothing has grown from the
garden.

not for a long time.

it's tiring work.

and each evening,
the setting sky
looks like spilled blood.

looks like letting go.

perhaps this is what
we need.

blood moon

concept: the moon sheds its skin
and resembles blood.

in the middle of the night
we are tongue-tied.

we are tug-of-war
blistering with necessity.

we have been here a while.

because all of the metaphors
groan with age. all of the
metaphors have sharp claws
and teeth.

this is a storm without pause.

and yet,
we breathe. and we breathe.
and we breathe.

and yet,
it still feels as if
there isn't enough air.

feverish

all of the notes fade
into the night.

they slim-slow blur
and we are left
with barely anything.

here, the city breathes on
and keeps on moving.

but our breath has become
warning labels.

and we turn into this unknown
analogy that no one thinks about
trying to understand.

as a child,
the dreams were sweet.

graceful like giggles from a tambourine.

but now,
every star has been stolen
from the window.

we have become strangers
(to ourselves).

we are feverish with need.

for patience. for mercy. for love.
for the hope that we are salvageable.

last page

i don't know how to start
the poem.

there isn't any skyline.

there are only strangers
and nightmares
that won't allow me
to wake up.

*you were doomed from
the start,* they whisper.

this is the last page.

only the night
is cascading.

only there is
so much space.

too much.
way too much.

i hope that
this is the worst of it.

dreaming about the world

we continue on dreaming
about the entire world /

even when it becomes too much.

anymore

meeting ten different smiles / each one
feeling like an accident / wanting to leave
these bones / behind / all of this heartache /
is a war story / there is a light switch /
but, you see / i do not reach for it /

funeral

almost as if i am trying to find
the joke, the laughter at the
thought of my own funeral.

it is a slow trickle. unfocused.
strangled.

the passing days have been nothing
more than a crime scene. some
stolen breath. a pressure point.

know that if someone were to come
looking, i haven't bothered to
keep the lights on.

or found the immediacy in climbing
garden walls.

(not for a long time.)

and i would just have to dare to
admit that i do not know what i am
doing here.

anxiety

anxiety has grown like shadows
on paper walls.

and with it,
i have grown accustomed to yelling
at myself in every tongue.

like being pulled from the surface.
like my lungs filling up with ice water.

and at one point you may come asking.
think once about it. think twice.

but the poetry of it all has
already been lost in the tension.

i have picked open the scab
over and over.

this is simply me saying
that i am not sure if anything will be whole
again.

crave everything. want nothing

out of every hollow part;

grief has been worn as the river.
all knotted up and tied around our
limbs.

we crave everything. want nothing.

in the evenings, when the storms
rise and run rampant, and everyone
startles awake, we try our best to
not let it show.

we try.

but we've forgotten about the art
of needing one another. of the
significance of what it means
to survive in these times.

the truth:

is that
i am still
learning
how to
comfortably
fit well into
my own
skin.

what is the answer

maybe i stick my hands
onto the steering wheel.

maybe i do it to crash
on purpose.

i do not always like
to talk about the blackberry
bruises. my hanging limbs.

yes, the walls groan,
yes, the floors echo,

this is the root of the problem.

but then tell me, when i speak,
what is the answer here?

i am my own island.
i am the white flag waving.

(again and again.)

yet no one understands the
language.

the world and the paper-mâché houses

after all this time, we are still unsure of
our footing.

it is the year of
withering roots and snapped limbs.

look,
the moon has changed.

once, a full hue
and now a sinking ship.

and grief?
grief continues to grow into a landscape.

remember how we once spoke
about the world and the paper-mâché
houses full of cigarettes?

it took us years to know that this,
this present way of being,
is all there is.

it is sad but some people reach their limit
before age settles them. do you understand?

we reek of battles.
we are gun-smoke.
we are hands on the trigger.

but look at us,
we share in the same heartbeat.

even when we are out of breath.

amen amen

but the sky bleeds /

weave and then / put up a good
fight / paint on a smile / remember
why we breathe faith /

in the middle of the night / fold
hands again / and we are all
amen amen /

we try / without blisters this
time / to carry love in every
pocket / instead of running from
the rising tide /

still / we try / we do /
ignore grief and its hunger /

amen amen / we tried / amen amen

stand still

i think about the rain,
and the space between.

twiddle my twig fingers through
each drop and whisper about an old
lover.

piano fingers, really.
the slow melody of constellations
that danced across her face.

sometimes flat notes.

but isn't that music still?

that following week, we had poured

like caving in.
like high rising tide.
that incoming storm off the coast.

prepare ourselves for the
aftermath carnage. because we know
that we can't always make the poem
what we wish it to be.

but that howling human in us.
we try. and slam into dead ends.

wind and then unwind our own bones.
and honestly, it's just we haven't
gotten used to the art of standing
still. of letting go.

at nine

if you were to go back
a few years, you would
find the little boy sitting next
to his mother on a plane.
it is their last flight back from
their first and only
vacation to tampa, florida.

on the eight hour flight,
he has fallen asleep,
barely stirring
on his mother's shoulder.

and right now,
the dreams are rich.
quiet for the first time
in weeks.

above the clouds, the sun
looks like sweet caramel
and honeysuckle.

gilded thread ready
to be spun.

but something catches the
mother's eye.

she wakes the boy.

look. look out the window,
she mumbles. her voice small, dry.
and the boy's eyes are damp,
groggy.

but he wanted to see this
matchless wonder, this

46

miraculous feat that had
caught his mother's gaze.

outside the window sat a bed
of clouds, that mixture of puff and
cream.

the sun dipping below
the horizon, the clouds
bathed in rich gold.

at nine, being this high up,
the little boy expected to see
God and his glory.

his throne and his angels
and his sovereignty.

at nine, he expected to hear
the sweetest of melodies and see
the floating of soft feathers and
perhaps glimpse his heavenly
father waving back as they
continued on their long trek
home.

but at nine, the little boy's
eyes only saw endless expanse.

row and rows of gold spun
poppies.

and the excitement was fleeting.

he turned back towards his
mother, her tired smile
never wavering. but there
was a glint of light in her eyes
and it was dying.

at nine, the little boy
knew that he could only
simply close his own eyes

and slip back into
a voided sleep.

it does not

in this instance,
the rain has been both
the music and the storm.

the blush and the unspoken
metaphors.

a dimly lit room.

a train wreck.

the truth is that we are only
barely hanging on in between
those claps of thunder.

tidal waves, really.

when it rains and our mouths
open,

blood spills.

and it is all sharp edges and
bruised fingers.

but these downpours,
they can all be a type of cleansing.

or an apology that we just haven't
gotten right yet.

if nothing else, we are still bone.
and learning that blood does not
always have to mean war.

learned vs. taught

my father didn't want a
relationship with me because

he thought i was gay.

so,

i thought God didn't want a
relationship with me because

i was gay.

concept:

a concept: overthinking. what would
you say if i told you that the quiet
grows like a continent?
like the night, haunting and expanding?
running ink? if i were to admit that it is
the stillness that i seek?

a concept: or something about being
an open-ended question. something
about reeking of gasoline and flames.
(i still hold my breath when the door
closes. when i shut my eyes.)

a concept: so i dream about skipping
town. it is already half past morning.
but nothing about this day is solid. and
everything is belly-deep tension.
storm and wet and angry.
and everything, *everything*
leaves a mark.

a concept: i wash my hands over and
over. i color myself with different
brushstrokes and careful precision.
but it is still mixed up. and now,
evening grows and it feels
parasitic.

a concept: i let go of the faith
like a crushed hallelujah.

a concept: i run.

prayer

this remembered space / the inside
of a reflection / a language /

even when lost / even with the
dark /

(as parasitic as it wants to be)

i just want you here / with me

if i am honest

it's just that

i haven't quite
found home
yet.

someone will say

i think, perhaps, somewhere
someone is whispering.

when i plant my feet
and become this
unmovable force.

when the words wobble,
when they become predator.

the times when we stand
blinking away both
the tears and the starlight,

we cease holding the steering
wheel.

listen, truthfully?
i worry about the red lights.

i never figured out the art
of building from the bottom
up.

but even then, perhaps, somewhere
i will hear someone say,

hey, wait. no. come.
come here. come back.

stay.

is there such a thing?

again, it is twilight. and the sky
grows rich like strawberry jam.

on the drive home, he is drunk off
of grief and shadows as thick as
sickness.

he doesn't know what to do. he is
his own gravesite. a plot and shovel
and the sounds of digging are the
beginnings to a plump symphony.

ocean tides of
sharps. flats. submerged screams.
and closed throats.

and Lord, won't you answer him? is
there such a thing as too much
human? he pats the tears dry. even
though there are more. even though
they seem endless and fill apartment
buildings.

but he drinks down the heat. (as he
always does.) attunes to the tires
as they wear against the gravel
outside of his home. and thanks God,
once again, that the steering wheel
did not listen.

gatekeeper

but what do you say,
what can you say,

when you are gifted agony
and become so used to
those wounds and struggles?

when it spills between your
fingers in hollowing waves?

or when the evening arrives,
took that greyhound into town,
and undresses us bare for all
the world to see?

do you or do you not
keep the light on?

look how the moon averts its eyes.

do you remain soft?
or do you become a gatekeeper?

do you begin some sad charity
and then watch as the rest of
pennsylvania moves on.

me, i stand outside in the
pennsylvania winter,

waiting for the sun to come
back.

waiting for that spring-thaw.

when wholeness comes

only sometimes, i let go of the
idea of wholeness.

i see the good
and pour gasoline.

i see the good
and light a match.

because when wholeness comes,
it is more rippling mirage.

more frost when it exits
my chest.

something intangible that i can
hardly remember.

when i see wholeness, grief
becomes a prick. a needle. this
aching point that lingers in the
back pocket.

but i stay. and i laugh. i try to.

open my hands and let the light fall
through.

because listen, when wholeness
arrives, i'm still not sure what
belongs to me and what doesn't.

my only hope is that one day, when
wholeness comes, it'll stay.

january

it is strange.

we have lost sight of
it all.

somewhere in the middle,
i guess.

or on the back of
the heavy shoulders of
january.

anxiety came and took
no prisoners.

pulled us by the
teeth.

it is strange.
it is so, so strange.

and yet,
we keep on living.

i am

mostly, i am here waiting.
i am all pause but knees bouncing.
patience on the edge of a window seat,
waiting for the moon to rise again.

mostly, i am some place else entirely.
deep inside the underbrush of a dream
that no one understands.

can words between you and another
taste like concrete?

i think so.

say that it all began sweetly,
like glaze dripping off of the side
of your chin after biting
into something fresh.

but then there are those wounds.

i know because
i grow thorns and prick myself
with my own untrained hands.

listen,
i know the light
but i cannot see it.

mostly, i am here
but some place else entirely.

waiting.

for a homing signal. for the
nightmare to end. for the moon
to grow full.

for one last miracle.

(run-on)

say i've rewritten the poem,
say i've pressed my pen to the page
twelve times,

say that the melody of the language
is all wrong and off-key

and the ink only runs down deserted
streets and the words only form
bruises on my lips,

which is to say
that i've found what i was looking for
but lost it

and you are somewhere across town
and for six long years these letters
and conversations have only been
one-sided,

which is to say that
this world, this world and its
endless pain,

and yet, its cold has yet
to break us.

Waxing gibbous

maybe

i have seen the door close more
times than the wild dreamer could
dream.

i have hit the pavement more times
than fingers have found their way
around the lock.

i have been swallowed whole more
times than the nightmare could
end.

but maybe,
maybe something good can grow from
this.

once more

let's just try it again,
okay?

let's just hold onto faith
once more, and go from there.

be brave

(perhaps the light is
hidden beneath.)

be brave
and trust the undoing.

even here

(or) alone, when warm exhales can
only scatter the autumn leaves. and
tears become rivers that swallow
the trees.

(or) yesterday, that love
turning into an ice age.
becoming water underneath the bridge.
a hollowed space.

(or) when evening arrives. when
feet stumble on the pavement.
fingers chase after a prayer. but
haven't found it yet.

(or) going off to sleep and the sky
above is still cracking. and the
thunder can only sit in your chest.

listen, even here in this
expanding dark,

there is still life worth keeping.

all at once

hear me when i say that we are
fading and blooming.

all at once.

i am still looking

these days i take my time,
sip lazily from the spring.

pretend that i am
the light.

(even though i am still looking.)

moon grows lavender

when the moon grows lavender. when
grief doesn't swallow the city.

when the night unfolds
but i can still dig my fingers
into the swollen earth.

when the doors open. when there's
more to the epilogue.

when you hold my hand
and hold my hand again.

and it all feels like a fresh dream.

sea of serenity

right in the middle of winter.

between the chill setting inside
of our bones and the shallow of the
moon and the dry, dry air.

we can still see it, i believe.

we can still bear witness to a
miracle

(if only we keep looking.)

what can we do

tonight, the sky is all landscape.

that unruly air, it is now mild and
tastes like eucalyptus.

for the moment, this is the clean
slate. the newly running waters
after all of the hard places.

a hidden jewel in the night.

and what more can we do but to fill
up our stomachs with gratitude, to
just accept these fleeting
moments?

lighthouse glowing

have you heard of this /

out of all / its broken parts /

glass cracked / splintering /

this heart / is still / a sailing ship /
lighthouse glowing / after everything /

somehow /
there is still one hand /

on the railing /

by grace

it is by grace
that my lungs

can still house
a story.

more conversations with the therapist

my lungs resemble now,
if not more, flightless birds.

barely expanding wings
to meet the skyline.

or the silver strings
of the moon.

in other words,
what i am trying to say is that

i told a story once,
but the sentences between
my teeth only felt like worn
leather.

splintering, hot and heavy.

but at least,
the therapist begins,
you've kept the story.
at least
you now know how possible
it is to live.

wreckage

an over-thought:

this will be a letter that i'll never
send.

and you may think it strange.

but i tell you,
the parchment will never meet
the mailbox

or touch the hand of the mailman

because the words (prayers)
have had a hard time
leaving my mouth.

yes, the pen still runs with
ink.

yes, there is still room on the
parchment.

but maybe, after all this time,
the pen has always been the weapon.

and i've been writing to you in the dark;
i've been writing with the wrong hand,

so each letter (prayer)
bleeds.

i can only hold tears in my
throat now.

and my lungs hardly rumble.

it is the art of
unlearning my own name.

of letting this ending have its fill,
to birth a new beginning.

of having faith that in this wreckage,
i may yet be redeemable.

rain

but then tell me,

what little possibilities do you
speak into existence when it rains?

handprints

in my dreams, we've given up
the need to smoke cigarettes.
to throw punches. to jump
from cliff to unstable cliff.

in fact, we don't even bat an eye
about the lost things.

so what are we left with,
you ask?

what will we wake up to
tomorrow to look forward to?

will our lungs still cage
that restless laughter?

will the kisses still taste of
plump fruit?

our handprints that have been left,
will they look like high mountaintops?

well, we are dreamers after all, you say.

in my dreams, we don't always need
to be the burning gasoline.
look, we can watch the petals unfurl
at our toes and witness the stars
wink their little eyes at us.

here, we are limitless.

black

everything is black.
not beautiful black.
brutal fist black.

the rain has come.
washed the pain out of
my hair.

but my mouth remains
unhinged. so the anecdotes
are muddled.

do you hear that?
do you live on street corners?

it is already tuesday of
the new year. and the art
has already fallen twice.

but still, i lift my hands again.
sip wantonly from the spring.

and try once more.

faith

to say i have become

more cage and storm.

more half past midnight unraveling.

more finger on the trigger.

it's true.

even though my lungs house
butterflies,

bright yet haunting.

wings plucked.

breathless.

still, somehow,

it doesn't mean that faith
no longer lingers.

what if

and what if your hands and my hands
became this collective library?

what if our fingers became stories
and tales about

the love, the breaking, the deep,
deep wounds, the overcoming?

spill

but i believe that
there is a miracle

always spilling
into something.

wouldn't you

wouldn't you say that these
beating hearts of ours

are brimming tales of
overcoming?

starry-eyed

getting by on the kind of faith
where everything isn't sticky-sweet.
because when the new year arrives
and you are greeted with nothing.
or when you make the drive home
and hope that someone has left
the porch light on for you

(but didn't.)

because the fuse blew.
because you forgot to pay
the electric company and prayed
that they wouldn't notice.

so you write a note
and curse yourself in the dark.
think that perhaps God has forgotten
his promise or had his fingers crossed
behind his back the entire time.

but you fumble,
listen to the stark-quiet
and light a candle instead.

perhaps faith isn't so much
of an illusion but more
of this starry-eyed promise.

this

in this, the hard
underbelly of the quiet,

keep on believing anyway.

allowing the glass to crack

hear me out. i want to know faith
more as the unwritten novel.
those metaphors that can cause
bloodshed but at the same time
heal.

listen. everything here is messy.
and nothing works when i ask it to.

but still, i try
to gather all of the heartache
and turn it into a piano piece.
only use these hands for good,
you know?

to me, faith is finally being able to see
the moonlight slither across
the dusty attic floor after a three-day storm.

it is allowing the glass to crack
but not shatter.

it is a seat closer to heaven.

becoming

i thread my fingers
through the night.

and remember that
the moon has to leave
for a while, too.

so i welcome the quiet
as a guest.
let it hug my
shoulders as my
mother used to
do.

this is becoming.
maybe i am not lost
just yet.

just a little

all we need
is just a little room.

yes, just a little.

let it be

if our fingers should reclaim
anything,

let it be in learning when to come
up for air.

letting the juice run

maybe i'll pick up moonflowers
today. despite the chewing cold at
my fingertips. or the smile,

forced and chapped and overthought of

for the woman behind
the checkout counter.

and maybe it'll grow like six
o'clock daybreak. like standing on
its own two feet.

maybe i'll bite into the
nectarine. let the juice run
down my chin. without caring who's
seen. plant the pit like a poem;

hard and bitter and needed.

a seed inside my own chest.

and maybe it'll sprout like a
white rose between my teeth. like a
sliver of kept hope inside prayer
hands.

blossom

with the pain
blossoming and blossoming

so is new life.

desire

the gift is when
you are desired,

completely desired,

even between
the cracks of thunder.

full

and when the night comes, will it always feel like
a prison sentence?

here you are, head down.
here you are, a stranger to yourself.

once, twice, you've attempted to hold
your own hand.

your heart, a foreign stone. a drought. a desert.

you know of this agony firsthand. secondhand.

and yet, you dig your fingers into garden floors.
pull up cobblestones and smell honeysuckle.

you've survived this space before.
this night and its heavy weight.

but

your hands.
your hands.
your hands.

oh, how they are full.

never

it is an unfathomable strangeness.
or simply grace.

how the weapons had permission to wound.
but to never kill.

one day, i'll love you

and you can still find me
asking,

will the bruised knuckles
always mean war?

or the pointed edges that rest
against the skin of my neck,
will they only produce
bloodshed?

when all of the ache
are thrust into arms
and handled like sandpaper.

should i just simply
accept the grief
and its hunger?

the clawing?
the grabbing?
the striking?

its war-like tendencies?

no. no,

it will take some time
but i have decided to
feel everything.

my breathless laugh.
my stomach unwinding.

i can start from scratch.
open my eyes again.

somehow, i am still alive.

the day is coming.
and one day,

one day, i will love you, william.

we are not

it isn't too late // or too messy //

to continue to reach through the night //

to let it be sugar on our tongue //

yes // there are wounds //

but we are not conquered by them //

enough

or perhaps it is / only ever after midnight /

or do you know / can't you hear it /

the hands wringing / the snapping joints /

after each blow /

we have let the world take and steal us
from ourselves /

from our sweaty palms /

enough now /

let this be / a new beginning / an
opening of petals /

spring / and vibrant / and beauty

eclipse

what a victory it will be
to taste the light again.

light

like light / like whispers /

we sift through / folded corners /
echoes / and rivers / that no one
dare touch anymore /

like light / sometimes /

we are just swallowed whole /
absentmindedly / and yet /

we are still here / trying
to fill rooms / rearrange the
furniture / crack a window /

at least / one more time /

know this:

but let it spill down your
shoulders.

and know this: you do not have to be
ready in order to be courageous.

we can

listen closely / we can still hear
the dreams / i think /

those sweet, sweet sounds / those
that take our breath away /

like exhales

again, let me find music on my
lips.

let the prayers be like an exhale.

let me seek wonder in the hollow
of my chest. pretend that the
night's sky grows blueberries.

it's those little miracles after
all.

if i look hard enough, i think
that i can still find a little bit
of light pouring through the lace
curtains.

and if nothing else, i am learning
that i can hold both the turmoil and
the joy in the same hand.

drink from the river

this time, i promise to wake up
and drink from the river.

even if i am the rage
of shadows. of flames.

and grief is there tugging on the
hem of something.

hanging on has always been
a necessity.

there is space in the dark.
and i am pulling through.

this is the stuff of
survival.

we are

in this moment. of misinterpreted
body language. heavy rainfall.
power struggles. empty pockets.

when love no longer looks
innocent. the sticky hot summer.
unpaid bills. and that one apology
you didn't get.

and the mistakes. my gosh, the
mistakes.

full parking lots and empty grocery
shelves. the change and loneliness.
and when the world steals and
steals and steals from us.

*we are alive. we are very much
alive.*

buttercream

let your heart be the open
drawer. space in the attic. an
awakening. rosewater. spilling.
a name remembered.

let it be moonlight on a
windowsill. buttercream in your
chest. and three more miracles.

let it be a child's song.
motherhood. storm and outrageous.
a little fresh rain.

let it be vibrant. let it be a
new found road. the open
ocean. a novel.

let it be here. let it be living.

hidden in the silence

there is light.

hidden in the silence.
the hard brush.
the icy current. the only
guide post. those stolen things.

even here these things can
bring forth new life to the world.

the white picket fences

those white picket fences never mattered.
no, not to me. never to me.

nor those studio apartments
or the full bookshelves.

or the birthday surprises
and the hotel rooms.

nor have i ever cared about the gardens.
or the hardwood floors.

what matters, truly matters to me
is the intangible.

the miracle of an upturned smile.
those second, third and fourth chances.
the mechanisms of a belly laugh.

being wholly and genuinely loved.

collective hands

something about our hands
being more than just bone.

something about gathering
loose strands of courage
that have been tucked away
behind cold ears.

do you or do you not know
what it means to become
reacquainted inside of your own
skin?

the same and yet unfamiliar language.

which is to say
that we have chosen to use our
collective hands as a means to dig
new ground. plant new seeds
like the poem.

we are the lilies
sprouting from the concrete.

hope:

more solid than a dream.

love

love / hummingbird quiet / crept
through the window / folded its
wings / held my palm /

again

to know this faith as the kingdom.
full hands. a best kept secret.

in other words, i keep the essence
of you tucked away inside my
bones. i run back to you

again and again.

to dance

the gift of / embracing
that childlike heart /

and now /

only familiar skin /

that still peeks / inside
an open window /

and this /

this is learning / to dance
underneath the hue of the moon again /

a knowing / that this is a chance
to begin to live once more /

**homage to the novel, to dance,
written by stephen mcclellan*

grace

truth: even when the sky
doesn't open sweetly,

you can still find grace
growing from somewhere.

in bloom

there is something in bloom:

the mouth of a river. the crack of
an eye. a cup of coffee. the nectar
in a stranger's cheek. lips the color
of sunrise. april, may and june.
a smile. a memory. a child. a laugh.

me.

becoming a man without a father:

learning to be less loaded gun.
less bullet.

more gentle palm. more lily on
the mountaintop.

even while

even while in the distance, every
note sounds wrong and intimacy seems
lost.

even while there is only humid
heat.

even while you pick open the scab
or every hand feels like jagged
clay.

even while the roots are nothing
but grief.

even while the season hasn't ended
and it is still only tuesday and you've
cursed yourself in every language.

listen. and listen again.
and then call it a good life.

living

with grace
and spirit.

gloriously

to be gloriously alive
means that the night
will come.

and feel like an anchor.

a continent.
stretching.

these will be the days
of mostly indoor rain.

meaning we are both
prey and predator.

the language will feel
made up.

a thinly veiled whisper.

it is in the hardest of times
when we will feel most alive.

cross the water

your lungs.
your out-stretched limbs.

expanding.

the way that sorrow
cannot hold you.
the decision to rise again
after bloody palms.
or when the windows
shatter.

yet, you sing with the robin
fluttering outside
the crooked fence.

or on those midnights when
there isn't any moon.

and when you cannot
cross the water,

you find yourself tight-lipped
and all the prayers taste like
uncertainty.

but when you can still pour like light,
pour like light.

you are the home for bravery.

forgiveness:

nectar for the soul.
a still beating heart.

roots deep

know that even when
it doesn't feel like it,

faith can be found
hidden in the spine.

it is there.

knobby-kneed but
feet firmly planted.

stretching.
stretching.
stretching.

roots deep.

it is everything

when the depression lifts:

it is war turned story.

it is an apology to yourself.

it is looking at next monday.

it is bare feet in the garden.

it is the heartbeat of warm rain.

it is sowing new poetry

(for next time.)

it is finding heat in your cheeks.

it is ashes spun golden.

it is fog turned vanilla cream.

it is snowdrops in the city.

it is laughter like storm.

it is enough.

it is everything.

i find them

i say.
i say.
i say.

i still
search
after
miracles.

when i must

when i must, i

empty into valleys.

empty into fields.

empty into plains.

and the hidden trails.

and then
begin again.

consume

dare i say to take the chance;
be so consumed by love
until you can take no more.

until you are full.

survival

that exhale of breath.

doesn't mean quick escape.
doesn't mean full hands.
doesn't mean any more high tides.

but

what i believe it means is
battle cry.

what i think it means is
another whispered prayer.

what i am saying it means is
i am aiming.

what i'm telling you it means is
that i am firing.

because

what i know it means is
that there is still so much
more survival.

i stand up.
i stand up.
i stand up.

it's time

the eclipse is over.
it's time to shine again.

endings and new beginnings

look there,
towards the trim of the sky,
that gold light dripping.

there will always be a little bit
of sunlight welling in
from somewhere.

epilogue:

it is a vicious love. but it is mine.
unquenchable and courageous.

heavenly father, you've taught me
to trust in the unseen.

mother, you've taught me
the strength of perseverance.

grandmother, you've taught and shown me
what it means to live with faith.

sister, you've taught me what it means to protect.

cousins, you've taught me
the goodness that comes with change.

best friend, you've taught me
the responsibility of choice and given me adventure.

nieces and nephews, you've taught me
the true worth of patience and genuine love.

aunts and uncles, you've taught me
the courage that comes with hope.

owl's nest publishing family, you've taught and given me
the grace of what comes from holding onto our dreams.

to this day, when i open my mouth, i speak prayers.
this is a taught one, too.

ABOUT THE AUTHOR

W. Scott is an author, poet, performer, and creative spirit. He has written three books of poetry in a series titled *Bottled Messages*. The second collection of poetry in that series, *Notecards and Scrolls*, reached #1 on both Amazon's "African Poetry" and "African and Middle Eastern Literature" categories. He is a consumer of coffee-related beverages and a constant dreamer who, when not writing, can be found pondering what lies beyond the Pennsylvanian mountains that he calls home.

Find W. Scott on Instagram @w_scott_author or visit his website at wscottauthor.com

Visit
www.owlsnestpublishers.com

OWL'S NEST
PUBLISHERS